Child Life and Se

A Remarkable Message

Otterbein Oscar Smith

Alpha Editions

This edition published in 2024

ISBN : 9789367242599

Design and Setting By
Alpha Editions
www.alphaedis.com
Email - info@alphaedis.com

A FOREWORD

Sending this little book out into the world is like sending out one of my children, for as they came from my heart, so has it. My heart has ached for my children as it has been necessary for them to go out and meet the buffetings of an unsympathetic world and so aches it for this little fledgling. But still I have a hope that the world will not be wholly unkind to it and that it will find its place and accomplish that which has been hoped for it, in helping human lives and adding to the sum of purity in the world.

This little message grew out of an address made before a section of the Women's Club of the city and their request to have it published. I have not changed the literary style from that of public address, thinking that perhaps it would be more effective in that form.

You will doubtless find some striking and unusual statements in this message, but all I ask is that you will give it careful thought and that you will remember that these statements have been made after twenty years of careful study of the mysteries of life and that they are backed up by the best of physical and psychic facts. I have not dared to go into detailed explanation for want of space and so may bring down on my head storms that I might easily dissipate if I were but in touch with the storm maker. But let the storms come if they must, I will rejoice amidst them all if only I can awaken the parenthood of this land to the dangers to which their children are exposed.

Yours for purity,

Otterbein Oscar Smith.

Sex Hygiene

This word hygiene has its root in the word Hygeia. Hygeia was the daughter of one of the gods of the Classic Mythology, and was the goddess of health. Sex hygiene is then, sex health, or sex normality.

Is there special danger of abnormal conditions or disease in the sex life of children and young people? We must answer this question before we can determine whether our time is well spent in the study which shall follow.

To determine this we must make a brief study of the unfolding human life and note some of its component parts and their relative relations and values in the organism.

We can best do this by a study of the accompanying chart. The lower line of the triangle represents the body, or physical life; the left side the feelings; the right side the intellect. If body, feelings and intellect were equal in any human being, then, we would have a perfect triangle, or a normal human life. But this is not true in any child or young person. This diagram illustrates the relative relations of these three elements of being as the child advances toward mature life.

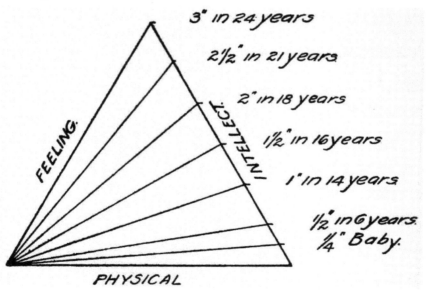

Note—For want of space the triangle is reduced from original drawing.

The early years of a child's life is almost purely physical and the physical plays a large part in the life of the girl or boy till they are well advanced in their 'teens, as you will see by a study of this figure.

Each side of this triangle is three inches long. The lines that run across the triangle represent feeling at the various stages of the child's life. You can see that in the early years the feelings and the physical are very close together and are the dominating impulses of the life.

The reader should bear in mind that the word feeling is not here used in the restricted sense of referring to physical feelings only, but to all the feelings which surge through the being from whatever source. We should not lose sight of the fact, however, that, because of the important part that is played in the organism during the teens by the impulses from a given nerve center, all feelings will be colored more or less by the outfloodings of that nerve center. As we have suggested, the child till well advanced in years is largely a creature of feeling, and what mind it has is what may be called a picture mind, or a mind for seeing things. How easy it will be for all the feelings of the being to become inoculated with impurity and place before this picture mind of the child such distorted views of life as will vitiate the entire organism! How important it is that a higher intelligence, that is the father and mother, create pure, noble and beautiful pictures and place them before this picture, or seeing mind, of the child.

A CHILD'S LIFE EXPRESSED IN FIGURES

Expressing the life of a child in figures, what do we find? As you will see, the baby has three inches of physical, three inches of feeling and but one-fourth of an inch of intellect. *This makes six inches of physical and feeling pitted against one-fourth of an inch of intellect.* The child of six years has six inches of physical and feeling and one-half an inch of intellect. The child of fourteen has six inches of physical and feeling and but one inch of intellect. *Even at eighteen the proportion is six inches of physical and feeling and but two inches of intellect.* How striking these proportions are when we put them in inches.

I would not, however, have you think you can literally measure a child in yards and inches or that they will all measure the same, for no two children develope alike, but in a general way this scale holds good. While you will find some children developing the intellect much more rapidly than others, and more rapidly than is suggested here, still you will find on the whole that this scale of relative proportions is not far out of the way for the average child.

I WOULD HAVE YOU STOP FOR A MOMENT AND GET THIS DIAGRAM AND RELATIVE PROPORTIONS WELL FIXED IN YOUR MINDS.

Think what these proportions mean and to what constant danger this child is exposed in developing sex abnormality if not disease. If an abnormal sex condition obtains it will surely sooner or later lead to disease. We may therefore conclude that our study is worth while and of priceless value to all young life.

The thoughtful study of this diagram convinces us beyond a peradventure that *there is vast danger of harmful and perhaps dangerous sex conditions obtaining without careful and intelligent guiding in the early life of the child.*

SIX TO ONE

Even at fourteen years of age the proportion of feeling and physical to intellect is as six to one. Where have you ever heard of a general who went out to fight a war with ten thousand men when his enemy had sixty thousand? He might make a momentary dash with such a force, but in the end he would be overcome. Still we allow our children to grow up with these odds against them and we seem to be entirely thoughtless as to the danger they are in.

THE MELTING POWER OF THOUGHT

Are you asking, why the human organism was not so constructed that the intellect would always be the dominant factor in the life? Had this been done there would be no possibility of the organism ever coming to perfection, for the impulses that are sent out from the inner life of man through the brain at the upper end of the spine are so powerful and so finely attenuated that they would entirely destroy the physical body before it has time to become strong and tense and able to carry them. *If the intellectual impulses of a grown man or woman were sent through the life of a child the body would be melted just as the fine wire is by a heavy voltage of electricity.*

God was wise in creating this sex nerve center, or physical brain, by which the organism builds and paints in glorious beauty and charming grace the wonderful machine, the human body, and makes it strong and tense so that when the work is complete the ego or spirit of man will have a perfect instrument through which to manifest itself to the world and perform its mission and live its life in highest nobleness upon the earth. Because of these facts *God has wisely wrapped the intellectual faculties of the child within its life, as he does the rose-buds in the rose-bush, that when the body work is completed, that crown of all His creation, the self conscious life of man, may manifest itself in all its glory through a perfect instrument and that instrument remain strong and proficient through the years.*

We may add this further suggestion to make our point clear. In our statement of the slow growth of the intellect as compared to the other two elements of being, we are dealing with the reasoning faculties and not with memory, which is quite another element and is not dangerous to the physical development, and may show a marked unfoldment at quite an early age.

IMPULSE AND VIBRATION

Having got these relative proportions well in our minds we may for a brief time give our attention to an important scientific fact which is necessary to our study. Our lives are entirely controlled by impulses which originate in various parts of our personalities. Sometimes the impulse comes from our bodies; again the feelings are in control, and at times the memory asserts itself. Then again the intellect is the dominating factor. OF THIS WE MAY BE SURE, FROM WHATEVER ELEMENT OF BEING COMES THE STRONGEST IMPULSE, THERE FOR THE TIME BEING IS THE SEAT OF GOVERNMENT. We are also scientifically certain, *that the more finely attenuated an impulse is, and the more rapid the vibrations are which carry such an impulse, the more powerful it is and the more surely will it prevail over the slower impulses carried at a lower rate of vibration.* A current of electricity of high voltage will melt a bar of steel.

THE FINEST ORGANS—THEIR FUNCTIONS

With the above thoughts well fixed in our minds we are ready to ask, what are the two finest and most sensitive organs in the human body and those capable of sending out the finest impulses? There is but one answer to this question. 1. The brain, or mind nerve center. 2. The sex nerve center. One of these nerve centers, the brain, is the instrument of the intellect and the other nerve center is the instrument of feeling, not of base and shameful feelings, as many people think, but of the most exquisite and beautiful feelings of which a human being is capable. *As the beautiful thoughts of man may be distorted into vicious and sinful things, so may the exquisite feelings which flood forth from the sex nerve center be debased and distorted into sins.*

With these glorious possibilities and purposes of this nerve center before us, what a horrid nightmare it is for anyone to think, as some people do, that this sex nerve center is the organ of humiliation and shame and is therefore not a proper subject of conversation in polite society. Nothing can be farther from the truth than this.

THE BEAUTY IMPULSES

Stop for a moment and think; from whence come the beautiful impulses, or thoughts OF HOME, MOTHERHOOD, FATHERHOOD, LOVE FOR AND PROTECTION OF CHILDREN, THE ART OF HOMEBUILDING AND HOME ADORNMENT? Come they not from this very nerve center? Destroy this nerve center in any young child and its life will be void of all these glorious impulses.

In place then of this nerve center, or sex organ, being a blushing, shame-faced spirit that mutins in the life of humanity, it is *the producer of all highest physical beauty both in the human organism and in its surroundings.*

THE MIND BRAIN AND THE BODY BRAIN

May I ask how many of you have ever told your boys and girls this? Not one of you, because you never knew it before. You have always thought that our sense of beauty originated in the nerve center, which we call the brain. The mind of man directs, unifies and co-ordinates and should control these beauty impulses as they flood out into the being, but they have their origin in the sex nerve center.

THIS ORGAN, OR NERVE CENTER, IS THE BRAIN OF THE PURELY PHYSICAL LIFE, AS TRULY AS THE GRAY MATTER, OR NERVE CENTER AT THE UPPER END OF THE SPINE, which we call the brain, IS THE BRAIN OF THE EGO, OR INNER LIFE. Through the sex organ, or nerve center, the physical life in its rarest and most delicate beauty finds expression, as through the brain the inner life, or ego, expresses itself in thought and will.

Do you ask for proof of this somewhat remarkable statement? Let me answer by asking a question. When are the birds most beautiful in plumage and sweetest in song? AT MATING TIME. *It cannot be said that this is due to intellect, but upon the other hand it is the natural upflooding of the beauty impulses from the physical brain, or sex nerve center.*

We cannot here enter into the deeper psychological question involved in this somewhat unusual statement, that the sex nerve center is the physical brain, but it must be evident to any thoughtful person that the statement is not far out of the way, as is evidenced in its beauty building power in the lives of the birds. There is an intelligence or consciousness in this physical brain, but it is not a self-conscious intelligence, such as functions through the brain at the upper end of the spine.

Because of the above facts and many others that might be presented, we feel justified in the statements we have made above.

When we contemplate all this may we not well pray, *Oh, God forgive us our sins of ignorance and false modesty and help us rightly to appreciate this, one of Thy greatest gifts to the human race!*

A STRIKING ILLUSTRATION

Let me bring to you an illustration to make this thought clear. Suppose you could unsex every child in this city under six years of age; this would be before the sex nerve center had time to flood the life with the sense of beauty. Then build a wall about the city and leave these children to themselves, simply supplying them with food and clothing, but keeping away from them, as far as possible, all human beings, who through sex impulses were filled with thoughts of beauty. What would be the results and what kind of a city would you have here in forty years from now? There would be little, if any, physical beauty among these people as they grew up, for they would grow slatternly or slab-sided, or fat and stuffy, and having lost the sense of beauty with their unsexing they would let the buildings go to decay and the streets grow up to weeds, and what a dreary waste this once beautiful city would be!

WHO HAS BEEN TEACHING THE CHILDREN?

Though the thought is new to you, do you not begin to see the truth and beauty of what I have been saying about this wonderful nerve center, or brain of the physical life?

What father or mother who may read this has ever felt it a religious joy to teach their children the truth about this wonderful gift of God to the human race?

I am not going to ask you how many of you were so taught, for I feel very sure none of you were. Scarcely anyone has ever been taught any thing right about it, but most, if not all, have been left to stumble along in the dark, as you and I were, and if by chance they happened to hit upon a plan, or stumbled onto knowledge, which enabled them to live together happily after marriage, well and good; if not, the great American juggernaut, the divorce mill, makes another revolution, and a wrecked home and two broken lives are held up to public gaze, as the result of its deadly work. There is not the slightest doubt in the mind of the writer but that a large percent of the divorces of this country grow out of the absolute ignorance of young people as to how to live together happily.

HELP!

But what shall I say? I do not know how to teach my children.

A most delightful book, which will put pure, noble, and instructive words into every parent's mouth with which to approach their children from babyhood till they see them stand at the marriage altar, is "Four Epochs of Life," by Elizabeth Hamilton-Muncie, M. D., Ph. M., Graves Publishing Co., New York. Let us ever remember that the education of a child along these lines should begin as suggested in this charming book, at a very early age, but it is better late than never, and if you have neglected your children before begin now.

THE PHYSICAL BRAIN

Let us return now to this wonderful nerve center, or brain of the physical life. When does it begin to send out *these finely attenuated beauty impulses, which must move at very high rates of vibration?*

These impulses which give grace, form, and all other touches of indescribable charm to the body of the child.

From the very beginning of its life to some small degree, and from twelve years of age they begin to show themselves the dominant impulses of the life. They rise in the body just like waves of heat on a summer day. *They are flooding every fiber of the being, giving roundness to the limbs, grace to the form, drawing beauty lines upon the face, painting roses in the cheeks, putting sparkles in the depths of liquid eyes.* All of this and more are these little builders, which we call sex impulses, doing in the years from twelve to eighteen. Is it any wonder with all this marvelous work to do, that like the sculptor who is to make a statue out of a block of marble, they must take possession of the body and become the dominant element in it? The heart, liver, digestive organs, and even the brain itself are subject to these outflooding impulses as they work out the beauty of the physical life.

Turn back to your <u>chart</u> now and note what a small part the intellect plays in the life of the girl or boy between the ages of twelve and eighteen. Just enough to be a willing servant of the sex impulses, as they work out the plan of beauty, as given them by the hand of the Master of all life. In fact the brain is largely an automaton in this work, for the ego has not had time *to fully lay through the brain that fine system of telephone connections and wires by which the brain becomes a perfect instrument through which the ego or inner man may reason out the problems of life*, so that up to eighteen there is comparatively little reasoning ability in the life of children.

IMPULSES MOVING AT RAPID RATES OF VIBRATION

These beauty building impulses are sent out in such abundance during the teens, that they fairly cause the body to scintillate, the cheeks to glow and the eyes to sparkle. Here they come, wave after wave, *like shimmering light upon the mountains, trooping up through the physical life like angels of the Eternal, making the body glow with unspeakable beauty.*

They should be guided by the finest and holiest thought, for *they are the elect angels of God to the physical life of man.* But what is done with them? Oh, sad! The parents have been led to think it is not quite the thing to talk to their children of these things and the child has not developed sufficient brain activity to reason about them and to understand them and translate them into elements of beauty and sacred service. Here the young life stands like a beautiful deer before the on-coming prairie fire, it feels the tremendous swish of the flood of feelings and physical life, like the hissing of the flames behind the deer. If only the deer can reach the lake for which he pants and swim out into its cool depths he will be safe; and if the child could creep, as it were, into the heart of father or mother and hear glorious, tender, holy words spoken of this flood of feelings, which is all so strange to it, and which sweeps up through its being like a storm in the forest, and have an intelligence translate them into God's own beauty of life, what a joy it would be!

When I see the mighty army of beautiful youth standing unprotected and in ignorance of the great danger before them, with no one to teach them and the very parents that gave them being, indifferent, is it any wonder that my heart cries out, Oh, sad?

IGNORANT PARENTS—RUINED CHILDREN

What usually happens if one of these elfs of human life has the temerity to speak to father or mother about these strange impulses? A blush of shame, perhaps, and the expression, "You better be thinking of something else," or "You should be ashamed to be talking of such things," ends the conversation.

A lady in high station said to the writer, when talking upon this subject, "I went to my mother a few days before my marriage and asked her to tell me about the marriage state. My mother was a good woman, but all she said was, 'You will find out soon enough.'" God forgive and pity the ignorance of such mothers!

Rebuffed at home, what happens? This child goes out upon the streets and from vulgar playmates, older than it is, through vulgar stories and suggestions, gets a base and lewd conception of all this in his or her life which God meant for beauty, for His glory and the glory of the race, or what is almost as bad, remains in stupid and dangerous ignorance till some vile octopus throws his tentacles about this dream of beauty and sparkling, buoyant youth, and the end of the tragedy is a ruined life, or what more often happens, two of these ignorant young people get together and because of their ignorance commit those acts against chastity which bring ruin and disgrace.

"But," you say, "such cases as you depict above are the exception and not the rule and I am not afraid of my child being caught in such ways."

YOUR CHILD IS NOT SAFE

I grant you this and hope by all means it is so. But do not because of this, settle back into comfortable indifference, for there are greater dangers than those stated above from which you cannot say your children are so free.

As children grow up in the home, if it is a right home, they often see father and mother kiss each other, and perhaps they see the mother sometimes lovingly drop down upon the lap of father and put her arms about his neck. The natural question that comes to the mind of the child is, "why does she do that?" No one has ever taken the trouble to anticipate this unspoken question and answer it, and the child goes out to mingle with its playmates of both sexes with this unspoken question unanswered.

The natural outcome of the child reasoning will be, if one woman can kiss a man and sit upon his lap, then all women can kiss men and sit upon their laps. Why not reason in this way? No one has ever taken the trouble to explain the difference between the married and the unmarried state and the rights and privileges that belong to the wedded pair, which rights are recognized by both God and the laws of our land.

Natural Mating

If you will observe them, children mate as naturally as the birds do. Here they are dancing about us like the sunbeams in the forest, in pairs of natural selection. You may notice them in the home, in the school and on the streets. Innocent little things they are in these childish matings and might remain so to the end of life if some kind intelligence were directing them. But no such intelligence is at hand. The mothers joke about these matings and tease the children about them and that is the end of the parents' relation to this gravest question in all life.

These children grow to fourteen or fifteen years of age and the impulses from the sex nerve center begin to flood themselves out in a perfect submergence of the life. They get hold of some silly love stories, that have been written by some heartless person for so much per line, and were never intended for any normal person to believe or think possible, but to their childish minds it is a chapter from real life, for they are not in any sense normal beings at this age as you will see by a look at the triangle. At this age *the intelligence is but a mere pigmy* in their lives as compared to the giants of feeling and physical life.

Seeing and knowing no danger in it, they follow out the natural sex impulse to touch one another and to caress each other. Why not? Have they not read in the love story of the lover and the sweetheart kissing and caressing each other, and furthermore, and *the strongest possible evidence in the case, have they not seen father and mother kiss and caress each other?* Is it not the most natural thing, under these conditions, for these children to enter into such familiar relations as will lead to serious consequences in many cases?

I know many a girl has lived through this period of ignorant familiarity with young men without having her character wholly ruined, and she appears before those of us who know the danger through which she has passed, as a living miracle.

But having escaped these dangers herself, what has she done for the young man with whom she has had these familiar relations? She has, unwittingly of course, multiplied the sex impulses in his life till they sweep over him like a fire in the forest. He is a manly young fellow and would scorn the thought even of allowing these impulses to expend themselves upon the one who had awakened them and increased their outflooding. In the midst of these experiences he falls in with some young man older than himself, and they talk it over. This fellow prides himself on being worldly wise, and so the younger man is influenced by him. The result is that he goes to someone who will receive him for a money consideration. Then comes the awful awakening, and he recognizes the fact, that the blighting leprosy of the sin of lewdness has fastened itself upon him. But after the first shock his heart is lightened, because some physician assures him that he can cure him. But that man is either ignorant or he is wilfully deceiving this young man, for the Almighty himself cannot assure him that this plague will ever entirely leave his body. God will forgive his soul, but no one can honestly assure him that his body is not damned for all time. It is true some men seem to recover entirely, but no one can give them any assurance in this matter. The best medical science tells us that these germs may remain in the body for years and then show themselves in various forms and diseases.

Is it not time for those of us who know of the awfulness of this dread plague to "cry aloud from the housetops," if by chance we may awaken the fathers and mothers who sleep in ignorance and false modesty?

AN APPALLING INSTANCE

Will it help you any if I tell you of a single instance, which came under my notice some time ago, and is but one out of many that chills my blood as I write. A young girl came to a certain city and secured employment in one of the business houses of the city. She was of inferior intellect and had but little chance for development of that side of her nature, but the sex brain, or nerve center, had done much for her and built in her body lines of remarkable grace, had painted her cheeks with marvelous color and given unusual brilliancy to her eyes. A foul miscreant, in the form of a man of older years, saw this beautiful human creature and decoyed her into improper relations with him. His body was full of the leprosy of lewdness and he imparted it to this ignorant young creature. But sad as it would be it would not be so bad if the tragedy had stopped there, but it did not. Think of it friends! EIGHT OF THE UNTAUGHT AND UNPROTECTED BOYS OF THE HIGH SCHOOL OF THAT CITY, WHO HAD BEEN ALLOWED THE FREEDOM OF KISSES AND EMBRACES OF YOUNG GIRLS, AS IGNORANT AND UNPROTECTED AS THEY, saw this young creature and were drawn into improper relations with her and the leprosy was passed on to each of them. This is not an illustration merely, but a statement of fact, for I had the facts direct from the physicians who treated these boys.

If this was your High School would you be alarmed? And would you cast aside your false modesty and in the name of God be frank and true to your children?

Though it may not be your High School there are always dangers enough that if realized should make parents earnest and anxious for the safety of their loved ones.

IGNORANCE AND A WRECKED HOME

May I give you a single illustration of the wrecking of two lives, through the ignorance of a boy touching these grave questions? This sad story was told me by a medical friend, who was personally acquainted with these young people, and while an interne in a hospital, in one of our eastern cities, assisted in the operation referred to.

A young boy of sixteen, of one of the refined and cultured families of the city, had grown up in ignorance as to sex relations and instincts. He was invited to a week-end party, at the home of friends, and while there, with a houseful of guests, fell in with a woman older than himself, who enticed him into improper relations with her. Whether she knew it or not, she was afflicted with the leprosy of lewdness and she passed it on to this boy. As soon as he discovered his condition he went to his father and told him about this incident and was taken to one of the best physicians in this country, who lived in the city. This physician treated the young man till he was twenty-four years old and assured him, so far as medical science could determine, he seemed to be entirely cured. The young man had become awakened by this sad experience and through this awakening learned of the awful fatality which attaches itself to this leprosy, so to be sure he went to another specialist and was examined and treated by him for a year. During these years, between the ages of sixteen and twenty-five, he had fallen in love with a beautiful young woman of one of the refined homes of the city; but so much of dread had he that he deferred his marriage for a year to make sure that the last vestige of the plague was gone. At last they were married with all the joys and delights of that hour.

Vain hope was his, for in less than a year after their marriage the physicians were compelled to perform an operation to save the young woman's life, which forever left that home childless and the young husband carrying in his heart an awful shadow which would never lift till the grave received him.

This is not an isolated case, for such tragedies are multiplied by thousands all over this fair land of ours. And the appalling facts are that a large majority of them can be charged to a lack of education by the parents. Thousands of dollars are spent to educate the children in books and music, but not a moment of time given to teach them the truth about this one most important subject.

THE AROUSED SOUL

Are you startled and does your heart cry out, "What can I do? Oh! what can I do?"

THE HELPER

YOU CAN BE FRANK, INTELLIGENT AND HUMAN WITH YOUR CHILDREN. Let me tell you, if I may, some things you can do. Let us think of the daughter first, but not because she needs more protection than the son, for God knows they are both in need of all the protection loving, intelligent parents can give them.

If the streets are sloppy and you want to protect your daughter, what do you advise her? To wear her rubbers, of course. If she has a cold and there is a raw wind blowing what do you advise her? Wrap up well and see that her throat is protected. Why do you give this advice? Because on the sloppy streets the feet are the points of attack, and in the raw wind the throat is the point of attack.

Why not be just as sane in dealing with your daughter when you come to teach her to protect her character and self respect?

At what points do these outflooding impulses of glorious womanhood manifest themselves at the surface of the body? The answer is self-evident, the lips and the bosom. You have known this all the time and you have sat idly by and seen your daughters go out into dangers far more deadly than wet feet or inflamed throat without ever saying a word to them about how to protect themselves. Why not sit down by your daughter of fourteen and tell her these truths; tell her there is a vital connection between the bosom and the sex nerve center which is more sensitive than the most delicate electric impulse and explain to her how wonderfully God has arranged the body of woman and why? Why not tell her the same truth as to her lips? *Tell her that unless God had made a vital connection between the lips of a woman and the sex nerve center she could not kiss love and nobleness into the life of her children during those glorious days of motherhood.* Tell her, with all the love a mother can put into the words, that will live forever in the heart of every true child, that because of these wonderful truths every *true young woman should protect her lips and bosom as she would the engagement ring, the pledge of love and approaching marriage.* Tell her, with the wifely love upflooding from your heart, why her father has a right to kiss and embrace you and *why it will mean the lowering of her character, if not its ultimate loss, for her to give these jewels of hers, even for a moment, into the hands of any man other than he who will be her husband, and as such has the loving right to them.*

Why not teach your son the sacredness of womanhood and the manliness of protecting it? Pardon me, if I say I am not writing a theory, but am speaking out of my own heart. I commenced teaching my own son when he was twelve years old and had my last talk with him a month before he was married. He grew up to be a clean young man and I felt a thousand times repaid for my effort when his wife came to her new mother a short time after their marriage and told her with such delight how thoughtful, kind, gentle and refined her lover was in all their relations.

THE DANCE AND ITS DANGERS

I may at this point call attention to the dangers of the dance. Every girl who enjoys dancing, and most of them do, should be shown the dangers to both herself and the man in allowing herself to be drawn up too close to the person of the man she is dancing with. She should not only be told that she must not do so, but told plainly and lovingly why. There may be nothing impure in the thought of either, for when they are dancing they are usually not thinking. Music tends to quiet thought and under such conditions they will follow the sex impulse and unconsciously draw near to each other, and they are far more sure to do so while ignorant of the dangers in it. In like manner boys should be taught to carefully respect the person of girls and told in a plain, frank way the truth about their relations to the opposite sex.

I believe, as a rule young people love to dance with the purest of motives. They are attracted to this form of amusement because of their love for music and the natural desire to keep time to it. The most zealous religionist finds himself patting his foot when a bit of lively music is played, which is but an evidence of the natural desire of any human being to keep time to music.

Is there someone asking, "If it is true that young people have the purest of motives in their desire to dance, how comes it then that so many frightful mistakes are made as a result of the dance?" I might answer in a single word, by saying, IGNORANCE.

It is the conviction of the writer, however, that no more mistakes are made in proportion, and perhaps not so many, as the result of the dance as by long night rides in buggies, or sitting in the shadow of trees in public parks. But the facts are more people dance than ride in buggies.

THE PSYCHOLOGY OF THE DANCE

The great danger in the dance is, to my mind, *a psychological one*, which might be overcome by knowledge upon the subject. Let us examine this thought for a time, for here is the crux of the whole matter. When your attention is called to it, you cannot think of more perfect relations existing between two persons for hypnosis, or hypnotic suggestion to take place than that which exists in the dance. To get this clearly before us let us note the steps taken by the hypnotist. He has his subject relax his body, and put his mind at rest and then he prefers to have soft music played. Under these conditions he most easily gets control of the mind of his subject.

Let us now study the couple dancing. The body must be in a more or less relaxed state, for graceful motion would not be possible with a rigid body. The mind is at rest, because the music lulls it into quiet and makes the dominant element in the life the feelings, for *we do not think music, we feel it.* Just here you must recall, that the sex nerve center is the brain of the physical life and continually sends forth the most exquisite impulses of feeling, which manifest themselves in all the glory and beauty of bodily charm and these *must of necessity mingle in their outgoings with the vibrations of the music and the feelings which it induces.*

Now you have these two persons, *with bodies relaxed, minds at rest, just floating over the floor, and carried, as it were, on waves of music.* Under just these conditions many an uninstructed and ignorant girl has passed under a hypnotic spell in which she has been led to do that which ruined her life and which she would have surrendered her life rather than have done, had she been in her normal state.

Let me give you an instance in point. Some years ago I was lecturing on the psychic question, and among other things I spoke of *the psychology of the dance.* The next morning I met one of the fine, clean young men of the little city, who was teller in one of the banks. He said to me, "Doctor I enjoyed your lecture very much last night, and I believe you have the right idea as to the psychology of the dance." He said, "Sometime ago I was dancing with one of the finest young ladies in this city, one who is absolutely above reproach. As you said, 'we were just floating along over the floor charmed by the music.' I was looking down at her (he was a tall man), and thinking what a nice young woman she was, when all at once she laid her face against mine. She did not excuse herself then and she has not apologized since and I do not believe she knew that she did it." This is the conclusion of a sane, thoughtful young man, as he pondered over an unusual experience with a pure-minded and irreproachable young woman.

May I here give the testimony of an educated, thoughtful young man of thirty? In a frank talk with me, he said: "There have been a few times in my life when I have found it necessary to stop dancing with certain ladies."

There might not have been the slightest wrong thought in the minds of this young man or the lady he was dancing with, but the outflooding impulses from the sex nerve center in the life of the lady might just at that time have been so vital and have been carried at such rapid rates of vibration as to make themselves felt in the atmosphere about her. This, my friends, might happen *without an evil thought upon the part of either, for this brain of the physical life may and does send out these impulses without the recognition of the intellect.*

Had this young man observed these ladies he would have noted a charming and unusual color of the skin of the face and an unusual and bewitching sparkle in the eyes, both of which indicate marked activity of the sex brain, or nerve center.

SHOULD THE DANCE BE ABOLISHED?

There are many good people who would like to abolish the dance, and because of the ignorance of the larger number of people who engage in this amusement, I think I would join with them, but in all probability we will never be able to do it, so long as people love music and instinctively keep time to it.

It may be in our zeal in this matter we are making a mistake and taking a wrong view of the question and by vicious, and sometimes senseless, attacks upon many good young people and this particular form of amusement in which they engage, doing both them and ourselves an injustice and keeping many of them out of the Kingdom. Of this I am sure, if young people are to dance *they should have proper chaperonage and a right knowledge of the possible dangers and how to avoid them.* NO GREATER

MISTAKE COULD BE MADE THAN TO ALLOW YOUNG PEOPLE TO ATTEND PUBLIC DANCES.

May I close this little message then, which goes out with a prayer for God's blessings to rest upon all who read it, that it may be a helpful message to them; by urging frankness and candor upon the part of you, the parents, with your children, and if you are uninstructed inform yourselves and put such books in the hands of your children as will give them pure, wholesome information upon this most important subject in all the world, and God will bless you and them, and in joy and thankfulness you will see them grow up in the purity and nobleness of strong, helpful men and women. BE ASSURED OF THIS, IF YOU DO NOT EDUCATE THEM THE STREETS WILL.
